DONNY'S PLEA-
Thoughts of a Cancer Patient
By Louise Watson
With
Deborah A. Lonergan

Table of Contents

Dedication..3

Acknowledgements..4

Preface...8

Chapter 1- One Ordinary Boy - What A Man...................................13

Chapter 2- You're In The Army Now!...33

Chapter 3- Our Years..50

Chapter 4- Donny's Reflections...68

Chapter 5- Becoming An Informed, Cooperative Patient................81

Chapter 6- Advocacy Options...105

Chapter 7- Support For Caregivers...137

Chapter 8- Financial Assistance...152

Glossary..159

Dedication

I want to dedicate this book to my beautiful husband Donny Watson. He was the best, most thoughtful, loving, caring person I have ever known. My life was whole when I had him in my life. He loved me because and in spite of my flaws. I could never have asked for a better man to spend fifteen years of my life with. He will be missed forever and always.

I also want to dedicate this book to my friends and family on both sides for all their love and support. Without them, I wouldn't have been able to do this book. Thank you to Donny's brothers and sisters for sharing their stories with Deborah. It made it more personable and showed what a wonderful man Donny was.

ACKNOWLEDGEMENTS

This book would not have been possible without the input from all of Donny's siblings, Cindy, Mary, Billy, Mel, Mike, and Bonny. I have truly cherished your support for both of us during Donny's ordeal and for me since his passing. Without your encouragement I would not have known how to start this project. Thank you.

Thank you to Christopher, Donny's son, for sharing the happy memories you had with your dad. He really loved you very much.

Thank you also to my family and friends for your love and support during Donny's battle. Words cannot express what it means to me for you being here for me when I needed you then and when I still need you now.

A special thanks goes out to Edward Ecker for all the support you gave to Donny as he fought his battle. Thank you to the hospice nurses, Michelle and Tricia, who were here for Donny and for me and who are still friends to this day. You have one of the toughest jobs anyone could ever do. Thank you to the staff and nurses where Donny had his treatments. I know he loved you all and thought the world of you as I know you did of him. He was just that kind of a guy.

This project never would have happened without the technical advice of Dave Ungrady, the proofreading skills of Mary and Richard Scanlon, and the editing skills of Zachary E. Lonergan. A big thank you goes to each of you.

Thank you Deborah Lonergan for all the time and effort I know you put into doing this book for me and all the painstaking research you did to find all the information for advocacy groups and places for people to go who need help. I know most people do not even know it is out there.

I know I am most likely missing someone to thank, but I want to thank all of those who have come in and out of my life. You have all taken a part in making me a stronger person and making me the person I am today.

Of course I want to thank my sweet Donny. I may no longer have his physical presence with me but I still feel his presence deep within my soul each day. His last wish to get his story out to other people dealing with the medical system resulted in this book. He wanted to help in some way so others could avoid some of the agony, pain, and confusion we experienced. Donny dictated his story to his brother, Mike. *Donny's Plea-Thoughts of a Cancer Patient*, based on that story came from his heart, the most beautiful heart ever to beat.

Sweetheart, we hope we have surpassed your expectations and have made you proud of this end result. Know that we all love you and miss you more than we can say.

PREFACE

Excerpts from the poem, "Just a Common Soldier"

(A Soldier Died Today) by A. Lawrence Vaincourt

He will not be mourned by many, just his children and his wife,

For he lived an ordinary and quite uneventful life.

Held a job and raised a family, quietly going his own way,

And the world won't note his passing, though a soldier died today.

When politicians leave this earth, their bodies lie in state,

While thousands note their passing and proclaim that they were great.

Papers tell their whole life stories, from the time that they were young,

But the passing of a soldier goes unnoticed and unsung.

If we cannot do him honor while he's here to hear the praise,

Then at least let's give him homage at the ending of his days.

Perhaps just a simple headline in a paper that would say,

Our Country is in mourning, for a soldier died today

Years ago a commercial with a well known actor stated something like, "if you are watching this, then I have died". The commercial gave a warning to stop smoking because the actor had died of lung cancer. Well I am not a well known actor, athlete or businessman; I am just an ordinary man with a similar message. If you are reading this, my time on this big blue orb has ended. Yet, just like the actor, I have an important message to pass along because I also lost my battle with cancer: pancreatic cancer. I want to share some important lessons my experiences with the medical system during the last two years of my life, taught me. This will contain a paraphrase of some of my final reflections, not to vent or place blame but to explain the sincere compulsion I felt to share my story to help others. As a result of this self-imposed obligation, a significant portion of this book will deal with patient advocacy, both personal and political.

Since I am no longer in a position to share my story, my wonderful wife Louise promised me to have my story published in order to assist others in becoming their own best medical advocate.

Donny Watson (11/29/59-8/22/12)

♡♡♡

    I promised Donny I would share his story. At first the focus dealt with the struggles of the last two years of his life and his battle with cancer. He wanted to help people with major medical issues become more confident in their dealings with the medical professionals. Information on patient advocacy programs for many different diseases combined with practical tips on how to keep medical records and prepare for your visits with your healthcare professionals fill the second part of this book.

    As I went through our writings and pictures of those years, I realized in order to tell Donny's story, I needed to focus on the whole man. Yes, my Donny bravely battled cancer, but he lived a whole life before that dreadful diagnosis. I also wanted to share how an ordinary boy developed into an extraordinary man who, in his last days, never lost his innate concern for the welfare of others. This concern for others started when he was young, grew during the 17 years he served in the United States Army and continued until his last days.

The first chapter briefly allows you to witness the development of a brave, pragmatic, self-giving man. The remainder of the book deals with information on medical advocacy issues.

If you wish to jump past the first chapter for the practical "how to" information, please go right ahead. If you decide to read the book in that fashion, please give yourself the pleasure of reading about Donny when you have time.

All in all, I wish you health and peace as you use this book.

Louise Watson

CHAPTER 1--*ONE ORDINARY BOY-WHAT A MAN!*

The Makings of an Ordinary Man

THE EARLY YEARS

Some of this has been written in the Past

The present is but a fleeting instant

Some will have been written in the future

And when I'm done it's all in the past

Some of this has already been read

Only what the eye perceives in a split second is the present

This sentence was in the future when you started now it's all in the past

The question is who cares?

The answer is you!

Because you kept reading it!

Author Unkown

Sunday, Nov. 29, 1959 was a dark and stormy night in L'Anse, Michigan. How do I know it was a dark and stormy night? It was night in Michigan, in November and L'Anse sits right on Lake Superior, of course it was stormy! Donny joined the Watson clan that night and proceeded to warm hearts from the very start.

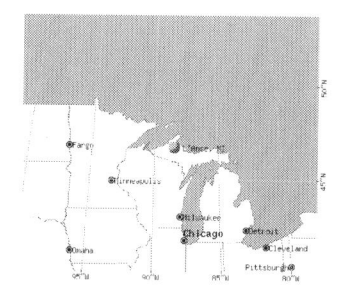

A house bursting at the seams with adults and energetic children would soon welcome one more child to the brood. Marge and Bill, the proud parents brought Donny to his grandparents home to meet his older siblings, aunts, uncles and grandparents. The siblings Cindy, 7; Billy, 5; Melody, 3 and Mikey, 1 greeted this new addition with various degrees of interest. Melody and Mikey took a quick look to see what all the fuss was about and then toddled off to play. Billy quickly admired his cute little brother then decided to admire him from afar when he heard the ear piercing sound that came from such a small baby. Cindy eagerly welcomed the little bundle, even if he did threaten to break a few glasses with his high pitched wails. She soon found that being the oldest brought many new responsibilities. including changing diapers. Learning to change diapers certainly at the ripe old age of seven definitely opened her eyes and shut her nose! Older siblings grew up quickly in those days.

Melody, Marge holding Donny, Cindy holding Mikey, Billy

At the time of Donny's birth his family of four siblings plus his parents lived with Marge's parents, Oliver and Ellen Adams along with their three children. The Adams children Nancy, Lloyd and Bob although somewhat older than the

Watson children they still enjoyed playing with their nieces and nephews. Perhaps the cacophony of this extended family caused Donny to begin to not only develop his desire to help others, but also his overwhelming desire to avoid conflict and become a peacemaker.

This crazy dozen huddled under the same roof lasted only a short time. The Watson clan soon had a house of their own, near their grandparents. Maybe they missed the utter chaos of 12 people under one roof or maybe Marge and Bill just had big hearts, whatever the reason they soon rounded out their family with a puppy. The children heard their dad's car so they got ready for dinner. Marge had just gotten Donny to sleep after feeding him. She took a deep breath and started putting the meat and potatoes on the table. Marge saw the twinkle in Bill's eyes as he came in the back door. His hands held nothing but his lunch box and thermos. "What are you up to?" Marge asked. At that moment she heard a whimper coming from his pocket, the children must have heard the same thing. Soon Bill broke into laughter as his family surrounded him trying to get a look at the noise maker. "I thought we could use a little excitement around here. Things seem to be getting too quiet." He reached into his pocket and presented a tiny puppy to the bunch of grasping hands. The puppy whimpered but eventually warmed to the overwhelming welcome it received. The children decided to call her Peanut, since she fit into their dad's pocket. Needless to say, dinner waited for a while that night but no one seemed to care.

Bill, the father of the Watson clan moved the family often. His chosen profession of roofing and siding meant he traveled to where he could find work. He often followed the path of major hurricanes or other natural disasters. Some men in that profession would plant their families in one spot and then travel to the job by themselves. This would mean living alone for months at a time. Family meant too much for Bill to consider that option. He would travel to the job site, find a home for his family and move them. At times they may have felt like a band of gypsies and the exact chronology of the moves have been lost with waxing and waning of life. At various times they lived in various states ranging from Michigan to Pennsylvania to Florida to Louisiana, and finally back to Pennsylvania where they settled. The children realized the importance of family because Bill would go to such lengths just so they would be together. Donny never forgot that lesson no matter where he lived.

During the time before Donny started kindergarten Bill's business flourished and Marge enjoyed the role of homemaker and the luxury of having a TV. While the older siblings attended school Donny would stay home and help his mom with the daily chores. Their time did not consist of all work and no play. "Donny, it's time for Jack LaLanne!" Each morning at 9:00 Marge and Donny would exercise with "The Godfather of Fitness". "Mommy, I'm going to have muscles just like him soon. Look how big my muscles are now." When the older children came home Marge would brag about how Donny had helped her get all her chores finished and Donny would show off his new muscles.

Donny

During all these various moves the children continued to grow and mature. One of the stories all the siblings like to share involves younger brother, Donny caring for older brother Mikey. The incident took place while they lived in Florida. Mike's words tell it best.

> When Donny and I were very young, maybe 5 or 6, we lived in Florida along the Gulf coast. One day our father had taken us to a shopping center and parked the car so he could run in quickly and pick up something. Well...he must have forgotten to put the car in park because when he got into the store the car began to roll backwards. I started screaming crying in utter panic that we were going to die! I was sure we were going to plunge into the Gulf of Mexico and drown! Luckily, a man in the parking lot saw us rolling back (actually he probably heard me screaming). This stranger quickly dropped his ice cream cone and jumped in the car

and put it in park! Meanwhile the whole time I'm screaming my head off, Donny (my younger brother) is patting me on the shoulder saying, "It's okay, Nikey, (his way of saying Mikey) it'll be alright."

Donny never shied away from a challenge even as a little guy, if Mikey could do it so could he. It reminds me of the old Broadway song from *Annie Get Your Gun*, "Anything You Can Do". While in Florida Mikey had a habit of greeting his dad by grabbing the handle of the car and riding it a few feet until his dad stopped. Of course Donny had to try it; unfortunately it did not turn out to be one of his triumphant moments. Donny ended up with a huge cut and a long lecture. This did not keep him down for long, he soon returned to playing with Mikey developing new adventures for their GI Joe and Johnny West action figures.

When Donny entered Kindergarten Marge began to help Bill make ends meet when business slowed down. Both of them adapted to the available job market and held many different jobs over the years. Roofing and Siding work, like any other outside contracting work depended on the weather. When the seasons changed often the job market did also. Bill liked his independence but he willing tried factory work for a time. He stayed long enough to pay the bills, and then returned to roofing and siding. While living in Florida, when things got slow for his business he took a job working on a fishing boat. He really enjoyed that, maybe it reminded him of his time in the navy. Marge, never one to slouch took jobs as needed often working as a waitress. She worked in a sewing factory and even worked as a hotel maid. Both parents passed down their strong work ethic to their children.

As the daring duo of Mikey and Donny grew so did their adventures. Instead of developing adventures for their action figures, Mikey and Donny played out their adventures. While in Louisiana they became superheroes in their Batman and Superman costumes. They developed a system to help the local police in case of a neighborhood robbery. They would put piles of mud on cardboard then placed the cardboard in the middle of the road. As cars drove over the mud and cardboard it would leave a tire print. The amateur sleuths thought that they could assist the police by having tire prints of all the vehicles in the area. All the police would have to do is match the tire print to the tire and they would have their culprit.

The rest of the children also grew and so did their responsibilities. Cindy being the oldest had the dubious privilege of being the built in babysitter. Generally speaking this often causes problems with siblings, especially the next in line because they don't like being bossed around by someone only a year or two older than them. Problems happened and solutions abounded, bribery with M & M's usually worked with the younger ones, especially Donny. The other two boys were not as quickly appeased. Melody usually just played at her girlfriends' houses and stayed away from any altercations.

Left to right
Cindy, Billy, Melody in Back; Mikey and Donny in Front

During one of these babysitting sessions Billy learned a valuable lesson, but not from Cindy he learned it from Donny. Frequent moves sometimes made school time difficult. Billy had had one of those difficult days at school, only to arrive home to find his sister in charge again. Then Mikey, 6 years old at the time started his usual teasing with Billy it didn't turn into the normal playful wrestling. That day Billy had all he could take and Mikey's mockery became the proverbial last straw. This time Billy about 5 years older than Mikey actually hurt his little brother. Seeing this 5 year old Donny stepped in and started taunting Billy and running around him in circles trying to draw Billy's attention away from Mikey. Donny wouldn't stop until Billy stopped beating up Mikey. Donny's actions caused Billy to step back and look at his younger brothers. On that day Billy realized that Donny had taken over what should have been his role as the big brother. Billy changed that day from bullying his little brothers to protecting them. That night at bedtime Billy gave Donny and Mikey a huge heartfelt hug and silently pledged to be the best big brother he could in the future.

Donny's will of steel showed at an early age as well as his creative side. Around eight years old he shared a story idea with Mikey. As they filled the coal stoker in their basement Donny laid out his story line for "The Eye of the Cat". The size of Godzilla, the cat could shoot lasers from its eyes. Like Godzilla, the cat threatened the very existence of humanity. Only on the brink of destruction did the citizens of the world discover how to destroy this cat. A mirror the size of a house became the secret weapon because it would reflect the laser beams back into the eyes of the crazed feline. Mikey longed to be a writer but he had difficulties coming up with ideas. Since this crazed cat story sounded interesting he asked Donny if he planned on writing it. Donny said he probably would never write it. Mikey wanting to act like the intelligent older brother offered to buy the rights to the story. He offered Donny everything he could think of doing his chores, a year's allowance, homework, even a free copy of the published book. Donny wouldn't budge. This obstinate trait would grow along with him and became something only the seasoning of age could mellow.

    The amazing duo of Mikey and Donny went from superheroes to Cub Scouts, and then onto Boy Scouts. Because of their dad's work schedule Marge their mom, did most of the work to help them earn Merit Badges. Camping with the scouts became one of their favorite activities. The Weatherly Hill Climb definitely became the most anticipated and memorable camp outs each year. For two days in June and two days in September individual racers test their driving skills by following the treacherous, winding course of one of the local roads spanning a hill with the approximate elevation of 340 feet. They compete individually against the clock. This event brings people from all areas so many of the local non-profit organizations set up food stands to help their annual budgets.

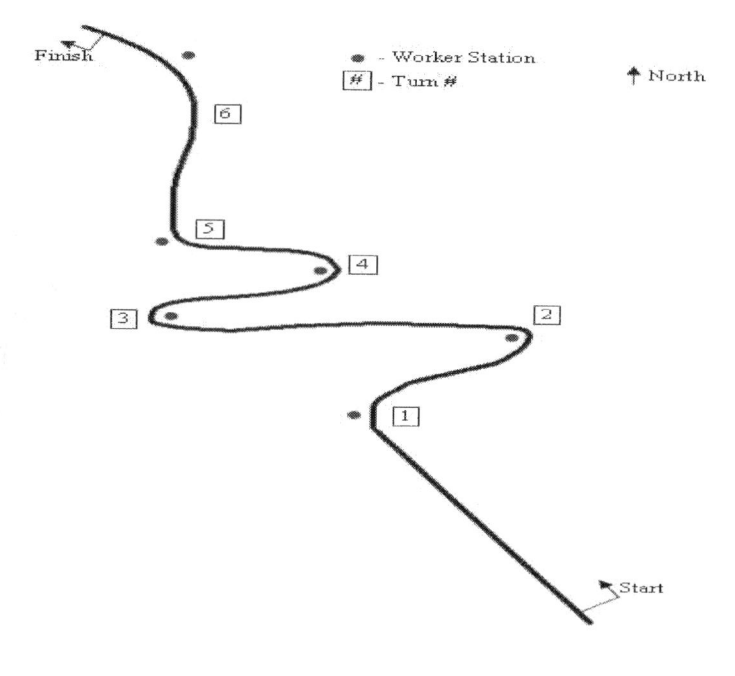

When the super duo grew old enough to camp out with the other scouts Mike had also grown old enough to request that Mikey no longer be used as his name. One particular year Mike and Donny set up camp with the other scouts. Now pre-teens the boys enjoyed their time away from home. After a long day of selling food the scouts all settled down about 11:00 for the night. Suddenly a screeching, eerie noise filled the air. No one recognized the strange blare and no one wanted to brave the dark and figure out the source of this ear piercing sound. No one except Donny; he ventured into the darkness until he came upon the source of the noise. He laughed as he told the other scouts, many of them older than he, that the noise came from the foundry nearby. The shrill siren marked the end of the shift. A quote by Henry Miller comes to mind, "*The ordinary man is involved in action, the hero acts; an immense difference.*" Chronologically, Donny may not as yet have achieved manhood but to Mike and the other scouts camped out that night he became their hero.

Mike didn't say anything at the time but he filed that incident under Donny "What a Man" happenings.

There would be other such happenings like the time Mike and Donny worked with their dad at the ripe old age of 12 and 13. They had the job of cleaning wooden shingles off a roof. Donny decided he and Mike were not being paid enough and he suggested to Mike that they should go on strike. Being a typical 12 year old boy who knows everything, Donny also suggested they ask for a raise and if they didn't get it they should quit. Well they asked for the raise but didn't get it. Donny quit, Mike didn't; yet another incident for Mike's "What a Man" file.

Donny

Besides Boy Scouts and sometimes working with their dad Mike and Donny were involved in whatever sports were available at the time. They also enjoyed the Civil Air Patrol an organization spawned one week prior to the bombing of Pearl Harbor. The CAP contribution during World War II is amazing, considering the lack of training and that most of the pilots flew their own planes. In 1948 Congress established them as an auxiliary branch of the U.S. Air Force. By the 1970's the focus of the Civil Air Patrol turned to search and rescue, plus an excellent Cadet Leadership program. The cadets' grades and insignia correspond to the equivalent grade and insignia of those for the enlisted personnel and officers of the U.S. Air Force. Donny's love for uniforms and his desire to serve others made this organization a natural fit.

This organization still exists and they continue to save lives and build great leaders.

Mike and Donny participated in another uniformed group that allowed their creative sides to emerge, the Hazelton Drum and Bugle Corp. Eventually they were joined by their youngest sister, Bonny.

Mike and Donny also participated in their high school football program. Donny played on the punt return team and also as a defensive tackle. One day he strode up to the coach and told him he didn't want to play anymore. Nothing the coach said could change his mind once again the obstinate streak appeared.

Although his father Bill did not spend much time with the children because of his work schedule his values obviously made an impression on Donny. Bill knew what he wanted and found a way to make it happen. That strong willed pragmatic streak worked its way into Donny's DNA. From an early age Donny knew what he wanted, some called him stubborn. Whether walking off a job site at the age of 12 or leaving behind a confused football coach in high school. Donny didn't budge once he had made up his mind.

No wonder his mother signed the papers for him to join the army. Donny tolerated school he carried average grades but he wanted more he longed for adventure. His choice of activities from Scouting to Civil Air Patrol gave him a small taste of military life. At seventeen, when most teens busied themselves with finding prom dates Donny quit school and joined the Army.

CHAPTER 2-YOU'RE IN THE ARMY NOW!

The Makings of an Ordinary Man

The Middle Years

"Far from being a handicap to command, compassion is the measure of it. For unless one values the lives of his soldiers and is tormented by their ordeals, he is unfit to command."

General Omar Bradley

"I, Donny, do solemnly swear (or affirm) that I will support and defend the Constitution of the United States against all enemies, foreign and domestic; that I will bear true faith and allegiance to the same; and that I will obey the orders of the President of the United States and the orders of the officers appointed over me, according to regulations and the Uniform Code of Military Justice. So help me God."

As you may remember, 1976 dripped of patriotism. Vietnam ended in 1973, and the country tried to put that behind us with a myriad of Bicentennial celebrations. At the age of 17, when most guys busy themselves finding prom dates and renting tuxes, Donny proudly put on the uniform of the United States Army. Since Donny left high school early, he received his GED while in the Army.

His family beamed with pride at the sight of Donny in uniform. His brothers and parents made it a point to have their pictures taken with him.

Above: Bill, Marge and Donny, above right: Billy and Donny
Donny and Mike

Donny attended boot camp at Fort Dix, NJ. Donny became frustrated with boot camp and considered quitting. A thoughtful drill instructor took the time to talk with Donny about his desire to quit. This discussion allowed Donny to make a more fully informed decision. Donny decided to stay and never regretted his decision.

Once Donny made his decision to stay, as usual, he put his all into it. He received promotions in Boot Camp and then moved on to Fort Knox, KY. As part of the 76 HEM Company, he achieved the rank of Private First Class.

SOLDIER PROMOTED

Army private Donald L. Watson, son of Mr. and Mrs. William Watson Jr., 150 Kline St., Weatherly, has been promoted to the pay grade of E-2 at Ft. Dix, N.J. He will complete basic training there Feb. 10. Watson, 17, attended Weatherly Area High School before enlisting in the army.

Donald Watson promoted to PFC at Fort Knox

Donald L. Watson, 17, son of Mr. and Mrs. William Watson, 150 Kline St., has been promoted to the rank of private first class at Fort Knox, Ky.

Watson is stationed with the 76th HEM Co. at the army base. He enlisted in December, 1976.

He attended Weatherly Area High School and received his GED while in service.

Joining the Army to see the world, he got his first overseas assignment in Germany. He fell in love with everything about the country, the people, and the language. I remember his youngest sister Bonny telling me that while home on leave Donny would try to teach her German. During his tour in Germany he took advantage of the opportunity to travel to other countries. He found it interesting that he could travel to Spain or Italy or any other European country as easily as we go from state to state. While stationed in Honduras he and his buddies took a much needed break from digging ditches. No gym memberships needed when you are in the army.

Donny sitting with buddies , working out in Honduras

    Donny loved attending the family gatherings when he came home on leave. Everyone looked forward to seeing Donny, from his grandmother to his young nieces and nephews. Frequently Donny came bearing gifts from the latest exotic places he visited. Donny didn't care what happened during leave as long as it included lots of family time.

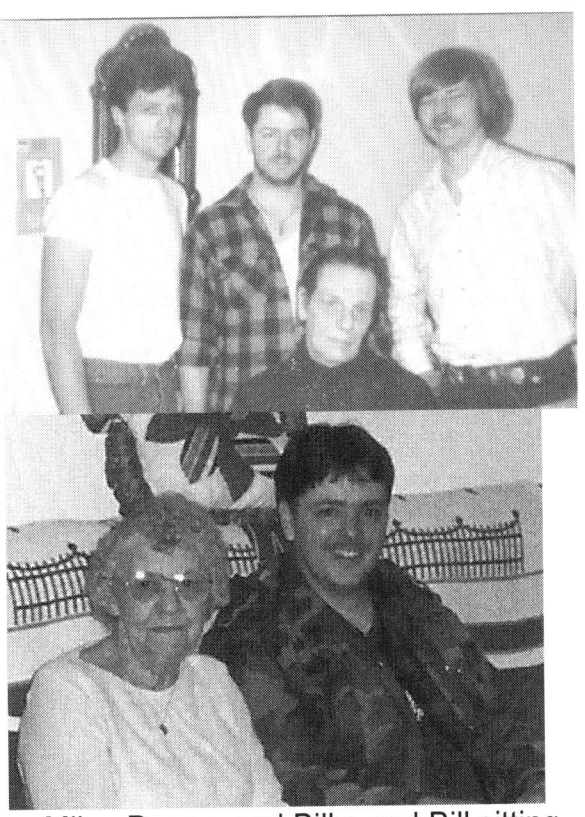

Mike, Donny, and Billy, and Bill sitting
Grandmother Watson and Donny

Marge and Donny enjoy time at the amusement park.

While Donny served in the Army, his dad continued to work in the roofing and siding business. Marge switched from serving tables at restaurants and making beds at motels to serving patients and making beds in nursing homes. The residents must have loved her smile and warm laugh.

During his time in Germany he not only served in the U.S. Army, he also became a Boy Scout Leader. In sharing his experiences from his youth he helped boys enjoy the positive experience of learning self sufficiency and leadership; two important life skills.

He stayed in the Army for 17 years; experiencing many different places during that time and attaining the rank of Sergeant. He married his first wife Jean in 1984, and she had their son Christopher in November of 1984. Family always meant so much to Donny; he always counted the birth of his son as one of the greatest events of his life. But sometimes life happens, and things change. Although his marriage to Jean only lasted about 2 years, his love for his son never wavered. He retained visitation rights and continued to be a positive influence in his son's life.

Donny totally fit the bill of the proud dad from day one.

Donny & Chris   Donny, Uncle Billy & Chris
Donny, Chris and Jean
Sitting on Santa's lap once again gave Donny a thrill

because he did it for Chris.

Chris remembers the little things they did together. Donny taught him how to play yahtzee (definitely an important life skill). Chris's Weatherly memories include swimming in the lake with his dad. When Chris wanted to know how fast he could run Donny drove his car next to him. Donny passed on the family tradition of watching the cars jump the hill during the Weatherly Hill Climb. Donny probably enjoyed this the most; being able to see the Climb again through young enthusiastic eyes. The whole family still enjoys these summer events.

Weatherly Hill Climb

Left-Right; Back-Front
Cindy, Billy, Melody
Mike, Donny
Bonny

In the late 1980's, while Donny enjoyed his leave Marge asked him to accompany her to the little town of L'Anse, Michigan. Donny figured they would just visit with his uncles who they didn't see often. Unbeknownst to Donny his mom had another idea. Marge needed the support of her most understanding son at this time more than any other. A few years before this Marge had been contacted by a woman named Mary. Marge had put a child up for adoption years early. Mary, Marge's second child sought her birth mother for years then finally found her through a series of interesting encounters. Marge had never told anyone of the adoption and although she wanted to meet Mary face to face she needed Donny for moral support. While Donny and Marge visited with her brothers Mary pulled into the driveway. Marge went to greet her then brought her to the garage where everyone gathered and said, "Donny, this is your sister Mary." After Donny closed his gaping mouth he warmly greeted her, after some adjustment time everyone started sharing questions and life events. More than anything else Mary remembers how welcoming Donny acted after he got over his initial shock.

After several years Mary made the trip to Weatherly to meet the rest of the family. In May of 1992 Marge's youngest daughter Bonny invited Mary to her wedding. As the family picture illustrates everyone in the family welcomed Mary.

From Left to Right
Back Row: Mike, Marge, Bill, Billy
Middle Row: Mary, Bonny, Donny
Front Row: Cindy, Mel

In January of 1991, Donny married for the second time; he and Deb remained married for six years. Soon after their marriage Donny's army unit got orders to deploy to Desert Storm. To the relief of Deb and the rest of his family those orders changed at the last minute.

Donny finished the last couple of years of service with the Army Reserves. Prior to his honorable discharge in March of 1991, Donny and other local armed service personnel were honored by their hometown of Weatherly. The town of Weatherly wanted to show their appreciation and pride for the service of their local sons and daughters. The local Rotary

Club joined with the American Legion Post #360, its auxiliary and the VFW Post #08128 to send T-shirts depicting the Weatherly High School clock tower between two American flags to all the service personnel stationed in the Persian Gulf.

Three Weatherly residents serving in the military received a locally designed T-shirt Fr evening in the office of District Justice Paul Hadzik, Weatherly. Participating in the event from left, Barry Gangwer, of Weatherly Rotary Club, project chairman; Gabriel Wargula, c mander, ANVETS, Weatherly-White Haven post 253; Donald Watson, Sgt. U.S. Army; Pat I denbrock, Petty Officer 2nd class, U.S. Navy; and John Kunkle, Sgt. U.S. Air Force. Also ticipating are: Clinton Kunkle, Jr., adjutant, American Legion Post 360 and Charles Parker quartermaster, VFW Post 8218.

After his discharge, he worked with his dad in roofing and siding for a while. Because of the seasonal nature of this work, Donny decided to look for more steady employment. He then worked in various factories over the years ending his working years at Hershey Foods in Hazelton, PA.

HERSHEY'S

CHAPTER 3-OUR YEARS

"Love doesn't just sit there, like a stone; it has to be made, like bread, remade all the time, made new."

Ursula K. LeGuin, *The Lathe of Heaven* (Scribner's)

"The Way to love someone is to lightly run your finger over that person's soul until you find a crack, and then gently pour your love into that crack."

Keith Miller

How do I put fifteen wonderful, magical years in writing? We built our relationship on a friendship that developed relatively slowly. I read somewhere that love happens when two people fill the broken pieces in each other. To repair cracked ceramic pieces, the Japanese use a method called Kintsugi (golden joinery). They use liquid gold to bind the pieces together, making it more beautiful than the original. That reminds me of our relationship.

In the fall of 1996, Donny had recently divorced and I was nearing the end of a rocky marriage, neither of us actively looking for a relationship. Donny belonged to a pool league at the Steel Creek Tavern, and I sang with the band performing there. Donny told me later that he heard this beautiful voice but couldn't see me. I wore a headset and mingled with the crowd as I sang. Frequently, I danced with one of the customers when I sang a slow song. I soon noticed that Donny attended every time we played at that Tavern. A friend introduced us, and eventually Donny became one of those I danced with during my performance. We enjoyed dancing and talking with each other.

My marriage ended in January of 1997. When we performed at Still Creek Tavern, Donny and I would dance and talk. One night, as the band packed up to leave, Donny handed me a note, signed "a fan." I still have that note, along with many other little notes and small gifts he gave me over the years. After he gave me that note, we started talking on the phone.

Months after our first dance we had our first date. We enjoyed a casual dinner and afterward, a walk. Then we went to the Jim Carey movie *Liar, Liar*. Each time we spoke, we became closer and closer. I had never experienced anything like it in my life. At times it seemed too good to be true. The day after our first date, I received flowers with a bunny and a note saying, "Of all the stars out last night, you were the brightest!" I couldn't believe I had found such a romantic man.

From that day on we were inseparable. I found he had a big heart, one big enough to spread his gentle style of love around to others, particularly his family. Family meant a lot to him and, unlike others I have known, he looked forward to family gatherings.

Top: One of the last pictures of Donny with his brothers and sisters and Karaoke with Donny, Mike and Bill. They were singing "Man I feel Like A Woman!!!"

Donny's love of animals brought us closer together. At one point we had two yorkies and two poodles; we took the yorkies everywhere.

Louise, Donny and girls

As our relationship grew I noticed that at times he could lose himself in deep thought. Rather than feeling ignored, I soon realized that when he had something to say he would say it. His youngest sister Bonny remembers their long philosophical discussions about religion and spirituality and other various subjects.

Donny kept copies of poems and other writings and pictures that touched his soul or his sense of humor. For Donny, good humor and introspection came naturally. He found no conflict in the two. So while one clipping would be a touching poem, the next would be an irreverent cartoon.

What a romantic man I found! On Easter of 1999, he gave me a plastic egg with a string of letter blocks that spelled out, "Louise, will you marry me someday?" Then my next present was a bunny holding a ring box with a beautiful blue sapphire inside. The next year, on April 29th, we married. One of the poems that touched Donny was entitled, "A Marriage Prayer", I don't know the author.

<u>A Marriage Prayer</u>

Lord, help us remember when we first met and the strong love that grew between us.

To work that love into practical things so nothing can divide us.

We ask for words both kind and loving, and hearts always ready to ask forgiveness as well as to forgive.

Dear Lord, we put our marriage into your hands. Amen

We both enjoyed traveling and trying new things. Both of us had always wanted to take a cruise, but neither of us had ever tried. We decided to start out slowly. Our first trip was to

Niagara Falls, and we enjoyed our trip on the "Maid of the Mist".

We decided to try the *General Jackson* river boat cruise in

57

Nashville. We got a chance to enjoy a nice dinner and a show.

Those experiences convinced us to try an ocean cruise. So for our honeymoon we went on a 4 day cruise to Key West, Coco Cay and Nassau.

Then we were hooked and enjoyed going on cruises whenever possible. Sometimes friends and family would join us; other times we would go on our own.

We were blessed to have the relationship we enjoyed. From our first date in March of 1997 to June of 2010, I could hardly believe my good fortune. We seemed to get closer as the years went by instead of growing apart like so many others. Growing old together occupied my dreams.

Then it happened. On June 13, 2010, Donny began his homeward bound journey. In July of that year, the diagnosis of pancreatic cancer struck me speechless. We had only been married a little over 10 years! This isn't possible, God! No, I won't accept this! Of course, those were only vague thoughts screeching in my brain. I sat in a haze, watching as Donny calmly asked about treatment options. From the beginning, Donny believed he would beat this enemy, just as he had other obstacles over the years. I tried and failed the "Suzy Sunshine" audition. No, my anger would not dissipate, I wanted answers. Why now? How did this happen? Why Donny? From the time Donny was young he was a problem-solver and caretaker. Instead of me supporting him, he supported me during those first few months of that awful experience.

    We had no idea what the next two years would bring. Each time we thought he had beaten this invader; it would rear its ugly being in some other part of his body. Donny knew what it looked like to fight cancer. A number of his family, including his mother, fought courageous battles until the end. I had no reference like this to fall back on. Of course I had known people who died of this loathsome disease, but that was different. It wasn't my soul mate, my entire reason for living! How could I cope with this? There is a saying that God never gives you more than you can handle. Well, I have to admit having my doubts about that saying when this started.

Yet as time passed I found an inner strength I never knew I had. I looked at my beautiful, kind, loving husband in pain and wanted to run away crying. Then I looked at his eyes and knew he worried about me. That's when I realized I needed to take a deep breath and smile and fight this fight with him. I could not let him waste his limited energy on worrying about me. The more I read, the more I found about the importance of having a positive attitude when battling any chronic or terminal illness. I always knew Donny as a strong, reliable man, but when I saw him fighting so valiantly, I grew stronger by his example.

One thing that happened as the procedures failed or the tests came back positive: Donny started making sure we would spend time with our family whenever possible. Often we would have impromptu gatherings at our house. Sometimes, friends, who Donny considered family, would come to visit. When he could still travel we took trips to see old Army buddies and other friends and family who lived far away.

Brittany, Christopher (Donny's son), Donny, and Louise

Too soon, the pleasure trips ended and our time on the road became solely for medical reasons. When I look back, I try to think of something more we could have done. Yet at the time we followed every lead available to us. We went for second and even third opinions. We traveled out of state. Whatever needed to be done we did it. Our major problem seemed to occur when we assumed the doctors were correct and that they spoke with each other. Then we experienced these trusted medical practitioners giving us opposing results for x-rays and other test results! We soon found they did not consult with each other! Here we are bringing tons of test results with us but no one talks about the results! Really, shouldn't these specialists come to some sort of agreement about treatment options? Experiencing constant testing with no consensus of opinion on the results just added to the stress of the illness. Donny got so frustrated, that's when he decided that something had to be done to help people who must navigate through the medical system.

Donny and I fought this incessant invader until the bitter end. I awaited a call back from Cancer Treatment Centers of America when he passed. That moment came at our home on August 22, 2012. Family surrounded Donny as "he slipped into his slippers and climbed the stairs of heaven" to quote his brother Bill.

And to the very end, Donny looked out for me. He and his brother Bill built a deck on our home to my specifications.

Eventually Bill finished the deck alone because it just became too much for Donny because of the excruciating pain he suffered. Bill told me that he remembers telling Donny about the completed deck and that he could let go now.

Friends and family often said we were a match made in heaven. We were soul mates. Donny became my best friend, the love of my life. Even now, I still have moments when I simply must weep. I have come to the conclusion that crying is okay, as long as I continue to yank myself up from those bouts of weeping. The world lost a beautiful man that night in August of 2012.

Since I am a songwriter and a singer, I decided to write my feelings in a song. I posted it on Facebook, and I'd like to share those thoughts and feelings with you now.

Forever and Always

By: Louise Watson

When we took our vows to love, honor and cherish, in sickness and in health, 'til death do us part

I never imagined 'til death would come so soon, too soon

We were husband and wife for only twelve short years, the best years anyone could ask for

If I had known back then what fate had waiting for us

I still would have gone through it all again

Just to be with you, just to be your wife

Chorus

You were that special someone

A rare kind of man

So kind, gentle and loving

Now that you're gone I'll do what I can

I was truly lucky to have you in my life

As my husband, soul mate, and best friend

You loved me for me in spite of and because of

And I will love, honor and cherish you without end

Forever and always

I miss you so much I still cry most every day and night without you beside me

It seems like only yesterday since I lost you, I lost you

I feel as though my heart went with you that August night and I'll never get it back

There's a void in my life that will never be filled

My world will never be the same, my world will never be the same

Bridge

Now I'm trying to pick u the pieces, trying to go on without you

I am sad, lost broken and lonely

I hold your memories in my heart; we had so much left to do

So until we meet again and I'm back in your loving arms

I will live on and be thinking of you forever and always.

CHAPTER 4--DONNY'S REFLECTIONS

The Flame Trees of Thika-

-Elspeth Huxley-Chatto and Windies, London

"*The best way to find things out is not ask questions at all. If you fire off a question, it is like firing off a gun-bang it goes, and everything takes flight and runs for shelter. But if you sit quite still and pretend not to be looking, all the little facts will come and peck around your feet, situations will venture forth from thickets and intentions will creep out and sun themselves on a stone and if you are very patient, you will see and understand a great deal more than a man with a gun does.*"

Although this is one of my favorite works and has served me well in the past, I realized, as I pondered these past two years of my life, that this is not the way to behave when dealing with a medical issue. My story deals with cancer, pancreatic cancer to be exact, but no matter what *your* story deals with you may find some similarities here. My reflections deal with my confusion and frustrations dealing with the medical system.

My final journey began on June 13, 2010. I had noticed some unusual and extremely uncomfortable symptoms. Besides discoloration of my stools and urine, I also experienced an insatiable itching sensation. These symptoms led me to my local hospital. The original tests showed a blocked bile duct, so I had a stent put in. In July of 2010, after several irritating weeks with no relief, I returned to have another type of stent put in. They decided to do a biopsy this time and found I had a cancerous tumor blocking the bile duct, but they told us it was not a fast growing cancer. Yet after more tests, they discovered the tumor actually sat at the head of the pancreas leading into the bile duct. Then they changed the diagnosis to pancreatic cancer, and a Whipple procedure* was scheduled for August 13.

Also called a pancreaticoduodenectomy, which is generally the removal of the gallbladder, common bile duct, part of the duodenum, and the head of the pancreas.

About a week prior to the surgery I underwent several tests. Around two days before the scheduled surgery, I received a call from the surgeon's office explaining that the procedure had to be postponed because they found a spot on my liver. They could not proceed with the procedure until I had received radiation and chemotherapy to shrink the tumor. I began to see an oncologist and had surgery to implant a mediport (a small appliance that allows drugs for chemotherapy to be injected and blood samples to be taken with a minimum of discomfort for the patient). By the end of August, I started the necessary radiation and chemotherapy treatments to shrink the tumors.

During this time I continued to work fulltime so I could pay my ever increasing bills. On November 4, 2010, I returned to the hospital due to shortness of breath, bruising, along with pain and swelling of my lower limbs. Although most of the tests came back "normal," I received a pint of blood because of my low hemoglobin level. The doctors did not know the exact cause of the low blood count, but they did have several suggestions; for instance, it could be caused by the chemotherapy, or not getting enough exercise, or not eating right or working the long hours to pay my medical bills.

In December 2010, according to one radiologist from the surgeon's office, a follow up MRI showed the chemo did work and the lesion did shrink; another radiologist disagreed. I became very frustrated when the doctors couldn't agree on the results of the MRI. Because of the disparity in the results, we went for a second opinion. These doctors found two spots on my liver not one as we had been told previously. Although this was another lesson in frustration, they at least took a biopsy of one of the tumors and it turned out to be noncancerous. We took the results of that opinion to our surgeon in January 2011. The surgeon still wanted to continue the chemo and not do the surgery. Since I did not agree with this I went for a 3rd opinion at one of the top hospitals on the east coast.

On February 1, 2011, we arrived at the hospital and I underwent the necessary tests. Since these doctors did not see anything on the liver, they told us they could perform the Whipple surgery and scheduled me for surgery on February 21. After the successful surgery, I remained in the hospital for 3 weeks. During this recuperation process I developed inexplicable complications, causing them to open me up in my room. They found an infection in my wound and decided to insert a wound-vac* instead of closing the incision again.

*Vacuum-assisted closure (VAC) is a sophisticated development of a standard surgical procedure—the use of vacuum-assisted drainage to remove blood or serous fluid from a wound or operation site--Wound Care Centers

I returned home and received visiting nursing care every couple of days to change the dressing on the wound-vac. Then a bubble formed, a call to the surgeon turned into another trip to the local ER to determine if my intestine had protruded through the wound. The local ER doctor diagnosed it as a fat bubble, not part of the intestine. Because the original surgeon wanted to check it also, the next day we traveled to that hospital, and he confirmed the ER diagnosis. By April 2011, my wound had healed enough to restart radiation and chemotherapy. Radiation occurred once every day for about two months. Chemotherapy occurred once a week until August. We hoped this would mark the end of the treatments.

In October 2011, I thought I could return to work but a severe pain in my stomach prevented that from happening. A CT Scan* showed a hernia so I had surgery on November 9, 2011. I planned on returning to work in January of 2012.

*Computerized tomography (CT scan) — also called CT — combines a series of X-ray views taken from many different angles and computer processing to create cross-sectional images of the bones and soft tissues inside your body.

Once again my plans changed when, in December 2011, I started having pain in my right leg. Both my family doctor and my oncologist felt a lump and the results of the CT scan and full body PET scan* showed a tumor in the muscle of my leg. Further testing confirmed it was the same pancreatic cancer cells. So instead of returning to work in January, I started twenty-five days of radiation and 6 to 7 hours of chemotherapy every two weeks.

* A positron emission tomography (PET) scan is an imaging test that uses a radioactive substance called a tracer to look for disease in the body.

On January 11, 2012, the day I began chemotherapy I had to go to the nearest hospital because of signs of a stroke. My symptoms included confusion, slurred words and difficulty in verbalizing my thoughts. Since the scan showed no sign of stroke the doctor said I had a really bad reaction to the strong chemotherapy drugs. This round of chemotherapy produced low blood counts almost from the very beginning. Because of the low blood counts the chemotherapy sessions were spread out to every three weeks, then every four weeks.

Around the beginning of April 2012, while still receiving the strong chemotherapy drugs, I started to experience back pain. Once again the scans showed nothing, yet my symptoms continued to increase in severity. The doctors prescribed pain medication and muscle relaxants, increasing the dose as the pain increased. On June 1, 2012 I went for a bone scan, which showed something that led them to ask if I ever had an injury to my ribs. When I explained that I did have such a history of trauma, they concluded the old injury caused my current symptoms, despite my history of cancer. Although I began seeing a pain management doctor, it did not alleviate the pain. The pain became so severe it started to radiate to my side and my legs causing me to walk hunched over. We decided to contact the hospital where I had the Whipple surgery to start the process of having me reevaluated.

On June 8, 2012, in the midst of trying to alleviate this severe pain, I returned to the hospital with stroke symptoms.

Contrary to my previous visits with these symptoms, this time they determined I had been having mini strokes since January. The hospital recommended I go to a larger hospital with better testing equipment and specialists that could better handle my case. The new hospital confirmed that I had several mini-strokes over the course of several months. We asked why the tests didn't show this before. They explained that it usually takes about 48-72 hours for damage from strokes to show up on CT scans, so if the scans were done before this time frame it is likely the scans would not show any damage. The doctors explained that the chemotherapy drugs and the cancer caused my blood to thicken and sent blood clots to my brain. So they discontinued the chemotherapy and started me on Coumadin, a blood thinner, to prevent anymore strokes.

On July 9, 2012 I returned to the hospital, because of difficulty breathing and tightness in my chest. After several tests, the doctors shared the ominous news that the cancer had come back very aggressively. The results showed the cancer had spread to my spine, scapula, ribs and liver. Several days later, the doctors returned with a dire prognosis that I only had 6 months to live. They started me on medication to make me comfortable.

My wife called the hospital where I had the Whipple procedure and because of my circumstance, I was admitted within a few days. After the evaluation, they told us I actually only had 2-4 months to live. They advised me to go home and start radiation to try to relieve some of the pain and continue the pain medication.

As I said at the beginning, I share this not to cast blame on others but to try to help someone else even in a small way. Perhaps my questions will encourage you to follow up and become more informed. Whatever you do, remember there are NO stupid questions. Ask for explanations until you comprehend. Ask the medical providers to write down, draw pictures, whatever it takes. If you have trouble understanding the physician, then ask the nurse or assistant if they can explain things to you. If you don't feel comfortable with their answers or their attitude, *please*, go for another opinion. A crucial part of your treatment and recovery depends on how comfortable you feel with your medical team. Look at all your options; get on the internet. If you don't have a computer, go to a public library and ask for help in using their computers. Ask your doctor for information on advocacy programs for your situation.

Get involved. Many advocacy groups have a political branch. Our medical system needs a lot of work; we must start to take more responsibility for the legislation that ultimately affects our bodies.

My final request of the medical profession would be to develop one standard protocol for screening labs, x-rays, scans, etc. I am not asking that medicine evolve into an exact science, but wouldn't one standard system for diagnosing lab and test results help alleviate some of the tossing around that I experienced? When there are discrepancies by the various healthcare providers on test results, work to develop a system for reaching a consensus between medical professionals who treat the same patient. Please, in the name of all your future patients, pick up the phone and consult with the other healthcare providers involved in the case when there is a disagreement about test results. A few minutes of your time may make a world of difference for your patient.

♡♡♡

You will find many advocacy groups listed in Chapter Four of this book. If you don't find a group for your situation, don't hesitate to ask your doctor for information. Get involved in your care; get involved in the group, as much as you are able.

If you find a group that offers third party assistance at doctor appointments, you may want to seriously consider this option. Many times Donny and I sat in shock, as the doctor explained findings. That shock does not necessarily dissipate quickly. It takes time to process. Sometimes a third party can help clear the fog, assist you in formulating questions and seeing your options.

We are beyond the stage where doctors know all the answers. We need to remember they are humans and make errors just like anyone else. Now we must work together to achieve the best healthcare possible.

CHAPTER 5-BECOMING AN INFORMED, COOPERATIVE PATIENT

Dr. David Arterburn, MD, MPH, Associate Investigator, GHRI, Group Health Physician, Internal Medicine, believes the right rate for any procedure should be the rate resulting from educated patients, in which "the provider and the patient come to a shared agreement," he said.

[Do you really need a knee replacement? "Decision aids" help patients weigh pros and cons By Courtney Humphries, Boston Globe Correspondent   October 22, 2012]

This chapter includes practical, simple ideas on how to become more knowledgeable and take more responsibility for your healthcare. This and the following chapters contain a lot of information I wish I knew before Donny's diagnosis. It may not have changed the end result but it definitely would have lessened some of the confusion and stress we felt while dealing with the various healthcare providers.

From the start let's understand that "cooperative" does not mean we will accept all things suggested by the doctor without question. Cooperation is a two-way street. When you present your doctor with feasible, well thought out questions, then the doctor should present the answers in clear, explicit terms, making sure you completely understand. Do not be afraid to tell them you do not understand; ask them to write it out or draw a picture, whatever it takes for you to understand. Always make sure you carry your Medical Journal with you to your appointments. Make a complete list of medications, allergies, diagnoses, and healthcare providers. If at all possible have someone else with you for your appointments. It is best to have someone without a personal interest in your case. If this is not possible, ask your spouse, child or another relative or friend to accompany you. Many times when given a serious diagnosis we go into "robot-mode" and do not fully process anything the caregiver tells us.

CREATING A MEDICATION LIST

One of the first valuable tools you can use in your new role as Medical Advocate is to produce a current and adjustable medication list. A handy medication list makes it easier for everyone involved. All healthcare providers, from EMT's to specialists, find a detailed list of medications and allergies extremely helpful. It also makes your life easier when filling out patient information forms because you can request that the nurse or receptionist make a copy of your list. Then in the appropriate sections of the patient information form you just refer to the list by writing, "see attached list".

This list may take some time to keep current but it will definitely make your life easier. Keeping track of medications your healthcare provider discontinued and why they were discontinued would definitely help in not taking something that did not work for you previously.

The easiest way to keep this up to date would be to have it on the computer. If you don't have a computer, you could go to the local library and create it on one of their computers, then save it on a flash drive. You could even ask a friend or relative to create it on their computer.

Of course you can do this in long hand but please make sure to keep it legible. This would mean rewriting everything each time a change occurs.

Below you will see an eight step outline for how to create this list. You can follow these suggestions exactly or adapt it according to your needs.

- Step 1-Your full name and date of birth and the current date of medications
- Step 2-List each medication, the dose and the number of times you must take the medication. Also list why you take the medication; cardiac, asthma, arthritis, cancer, etc.
- Step 3- List Emergency Phone Numbers for your personal contact person; also list all your healthcare providers' full name and the practice they belong to with phone numbers and

specialty. Include the name and phone number of your local and mail order pharmacy.

- Step 4-List your medical conditions.
- Step 5-List your surgeries: type of surgery and the date.
- Step 6-List diet restrictions.
- Step 7-List your allergies and sensitivities and list your reactions.
- Step 8-List drugs your healthcare provider discontinued for reasons other than allergies.

CREATING A MEDICAL JOURNAL

A medical journal will go a long way in helping you and your healthcare providers know how you are really doing, especially if you are dealing with any type of chronic illness. A medical journal allows you to keep track of your symptoms, physical and mental, in your day to day life. Think about it; how often do you go to the doctor for your routine appointment feeling the best you have felt in weeks? Then once you get in with the doctor you have about 15 minutes to describe how you have been feeling and listen to their new instructions for you. How often do you walk out of the appointment, get to your car and remember an important question you had for the doctor? Having a medical journal helps you remember your symptoms and your questions. It also shows you and your healthcare provider any patterns that have developed since your last visit.

If you look on-line you will find many suggestions for making a medical journal or diary. Sharecare.com has a rather extensive downloadable journal at http://www.sharecare.com/health/family-health/article/health-journal-personal-family-medical-information

You will find a very helpful article concerning why you need a journal and steps on how to produce one and what to include on the AARP website at http://www.aarp.org/health/doctors-hospitals/info-07-2010/why_you_should_keep_a_personal_medical_history.html

If you don't have on-line access then the outline below will help you get started. I would suggest you also get a folder to keep copies of all lab work or other medical testing you have done. However detailed you decide to make your journal, remember to keep it with you, when you travel away from home. The following covers the basic information. Feel free to make any adjustments to fit your personal needs.

> ➢ Step 1-Get a notebook, preferably one where the pages won't fall out due to daily usage. Designate this book for your medical journal only. If possible it may help to place a pocket on

the inside of the front or back cover to hold current test results you may need to discuss with your healthcare provider. This could also be used to hold new prescriptions you are given.

➢ Step 2-The first page will look similar to your portable medication list. Include on this page all your personal information: name, address, phone numbers, social security numbers, healthcare providers' names and phone numbers, along with your local and mail order pharmacies' contact information.

HINT: Don't write on both sides of the paper

➢ Step 3-on the next fully blank right page, list the statistics your provider asked you to track. Those may include your weight, blood pressure or even a daily food log; discuss these with your healthcare provider. You would also list any

89

changes to your statistics in this area. If you experience a migraine after eating certain foods, track your patterns here. Make sure you highlight important changes.

➤ Step 4-On the left page you jot down a quick summary of right page, noting any changes or patterns you observe. You also list any questions you have for your healthcare provider. Those with chronic illness may want to note those days when you are feeling down or when you are having a good day. This will enable you to quickly find patterns in your mood swings and other important changes you want to discuss with your healthcare provider.

➤ Step 5-You may also use the left page to note any changes in medication your healthcare provider would prescribe. Note when they want you to get lab work or testing completed. Also note any specific things they told you to look for before your next visit.

PERSONAL-FAMILY HEALTH HISTORY

A family history allows you and your healthcare provider a look at what diseases run in your family. The CDC website, http://www.cdc.gov/genomics/famhistory/ recommends you show 3 generations in your health history. Their definition of Generation degrees follows: "First-degree=parents, brothers, sisters, and children; Second-degree=aunts, uncles, nieces, nephew, grandparents, grandchildren; Third-degree=first cousins."

This history enables your healthcare provider to identify which diseases you are at risk for developing. Of course, just because you are at risk for developing a disease, doesn't mean you will absolutely develop it. This information enables you to begin discussions with your healthcare provider about adjusting your lifestyle to limit some of the risk factors involved with those diseases. Sharing this family history with the younger generations in your family will give them a wakeup call for how they should adjust their lifestyle also.

Perhaps your next family gathering can include sharing stories about the medical history of your family. If you are not comfortable with this type of conversation, then contact your family members by e-mail or use the postal service. Send what you have accumulated so far and ask them to add their personal and family medical information along with any medical information they can remember about those who passed. You can then update the information as major changes occur or send out requests for updates every year or so. It may be best to have one person in charge of collecting and posting changes.

The CDC (Center for Disease Control) considers this so important that they teamed with the Surgeon General's office and developed a computer based program to assist you in developing your history. If you want to develop your history in this fashion the website follows: https://familyhistory.hhs.gov/fhh-web/home.action.

I have included the basic information you should include. Some of the information may seem similar to that kept on your

Medication List or Medical Journal but remember this form is for you to share with your family and your healthcare providers.

- ➤ Step 1-Name, Gender, date of birth, were you born a twin [identical or fraternal], plus your present height and weight.
- ➤ Step 2-Name of disease or condition, age of onset and action taken.
- ➤ Step 3-Ethnicity [important because of some conditions/diseases are more prevalent in certain ethnic groups].
- ➤ Step 4-Build your family medical history one person at a time, following Step 2 and Step 3.

IMPORTANCE OF RESEARCH

No matter what your diagnosis, you need to take responsibility for finding out all you can about it and the current treatment options. Do not assume because a specialist recommends a form of treatment that you must accept it. Ask if there are other options available. Tell the doctor you would like time to consider all your options. Sometimes doctors and patients do not fit well together; there may be a conflict in personalities. The doctor may not be open to alternative treatments that you feel strongly about trying or at least considering. When situations like this occur, do not hesitate to get a second opinion or third or fourth.

As you consider treatment options, do your research in finding the latest treatments available. If these treatments are not available in your area, consider whether to travel to where they are available. Finding the treatment option and provider that you are comfortable with can make all the difference in your recovery or your ability to cope with a chronic disease.

Not long ago we had few options; we had hospitals and "Modern" medicine. Today, we have more options open to us and the following section will explore some of those options.

WHAT ARE MY OPTIONS

Most of us will like the idea of having our health care professional listen to our questions and discuss our suggestions for treatment. In order for that to occur, we must be confident in our suggestions. Organization, through the use of medical histories and journals, allows us to give the provider precise feedback about our symptoms since we were last seen. Research will give us the information and confidence we need to present our questions and opinions to our providers about treatment options. I generally use the Internet as my source for information concerning advocacy groups. However, whenever possible I have also included non-Internet contact information for your convenience.

Today we have many choices when deciding what type of medical care we want. Many people automatically opt for our conventional Western medicine. Yet in the past few decades, more and more people have opted for Complimentary, Alternative or Integrative medicine. As a matter of fact, this has become so popular we now have a government watchdog agency called National Center for Complementary and Alternative Medicine. This agency does the scientific research on all complementary and alternative practices that fall outside conventional medical practices. For those who want to look further into this agency the contact information follows. The following information comes from http://nccam.nih.gov/health/whatiscam.

> ➢ **NCCAM Clearinghouse** provides information on NCCAM and complementary health approaches, including publications and searches of Federal databases of scientific and medical literature. The Clearinghouse does not provide medical advice, treatment recommendations, or referrals to practitioners.
>   o Toll-free in the U.S.: 1-888-644-6226
>   o TTY (for deaf and hard-of-hearing callers): 1-866-464-3615
>   o Web site: nccam.nih.gov

- E-mail: info@nccam.nih.gov

➢ **NCCAM's Mission** using scientific investigation it defines the usefulness and safety of complementary health approaches and their roles in improving health care

➢ **NCCAM's Vision** decisions regarding the use and integration of complementary health approaches made by the general public, health care professionals and health policymakers will take into consideration the scientific evidence found as a result of their rigorous investigations

- Find more information at nccam.nih.gov/about/ataglance

HINT: Always look for reliable sources when searching for medical information. Look for a well known hospital/teaching center, perhaps a site for a medical provider with which you are familiar or at least a <.gov> in the address.

Let's try to uncover the differences and similarities between Complimentary, Integrative and Alternative medicines. First, despite many people using the terms Complementary and Alternative medicines interchangeably, the two terms actually refer to different concepts.

- ➤ Alternative medicine replaces conventional medicine.
- ➤ Complementary refers to using a combination of conventional medicine with a non-mainstream approach.
- ➤ Integrative health care uses complementary medicine along with conventional medicine.
  - o For example Integrative Cancer Treatment Centers may use acupuncture or meditation to help side effects from chemotherapy treatments.

The trend towards Integrative health care has increased, although there is little hard scientific evidence to support the patient's perceived improvement.

The NCCAM uses the term "complementary health approaches", which they break down into two categories.

- ➢ Natural Products-herbs, vitamins, etc., usually sold as dietary supplements
  - ○ Research continues to discover efficacy and side effects including interaction with over the counter and prescription medications
- ➢ Mind and Body Practices-include a wide variety of procedures and techniques. Some of these include the following:
  - ○ Acupuncture –certain points of the body are stimulated by the practitioner by inserting thin needles through the skin.
  - ○ Massage Therapy- manipulating the soft tissues of your body with several different techniques.

- Meditation (Mindfulness or Transcendental)-teaches people to learn how to focus their attention.
- Movement therapies- a variety of Eastern and Western movements meant to relieve pain and increase mobility.
- Relaxation techniques-designed to increase the patient's awareness of and ability to produce the body's natural relaxation response.
- Spinal manipulation-trained professionals use this technique to apply "controlled force" to the spine.
- Tai chi and qi gong-come from traditional Chinese medicine and use a variety of postures, movements, coordinated breathing and mental focus.
- Yoga combines postures, movements, breathing and meditation.

Naturopathy, Homeopathy, Ayurvedic and Chinese medicine do not fall into the above categories. These alternatives generally work alone and not in combination with conventional western medicine.

Remember, we are donning our Cooperative patient hats. That means we must do our homework and not just blindly accept cousin Suzy's recommendation that a complimentary medicine or practitioner that helped her will also help you. Each of us reacts differently to different stimuli. We need to take responsibility for our own health; therefore, we need to read the information available to us. According to the NCCAM we need to take precautionary measures when using Complimentary and Alternative medicine. The following lists the basics that we must consider:

> ➢ DRUG INTERACTIONS-At times natural products may interact with prescription

medications and cause the prescription not to act as planned.

- PRODUCT CONTAMINATION-At times supplements have been found to have traces of prescription drugs or other contaminants.

As with any other treatment we must enter into Complimentary and Alternative treatments with our eyes wide open. Use all the resources available to you to look into every treatment option you want to consider.

CHAPTER 6-ADVOCACY OPTIONS

"God grant me the serenity

to accept the things I cannot change;

courage to change the things I can;

and wisdom to know the difference…"

-Excerpt from Serenity Prayer by Reinhold Niebuhr

According to http://www.thefreedictionary.com, advocacy means "active support" or "the act of pleading or arguing in favor of something". These definitions leave no doubt that an advocate is an active participant.

When dealing with a chronic or life threatening illness having an active supporter pleading for our best interests makes the treacherous journey through our medical system bearable. There were many times during Donny's journey that we felt lost and alone. Donny's wish to help others not have to endure the same hardships we experienced led to this chapter. Not only will I deal with advocacy and support groups that deal with specific conditions, I will also give you information on a couple of foundations that help with all aspects of your journey from employers to insurance companies and medical professionals.

One of the first places to check for patient advocates is you insurance company. At the same time, be aware that the advocate's first loyalty will be to their employer not to you. Because of the possibility of a conflict of interest, a new career choice has arisen--paid patient advocate. There are still free options available, and I will discuss the national non-profit Patient Advocacy Foundation before any other organization.

Because Donny and I dealt with cancer, I will have a number of resources listed under the sub-heading of cancer. Once again I will have the resources listed alphabetically to make it easier to follow.

For each of the organizations mentioned their contact information will include street addresses, phone numbers, email addresses and websites, if available.

Patient Advocate Foundation

421 Butler Farm Road
Hampton, VA 23666
Phone: 800-532-5274
Fax: 757-873-8999
Email: help@patientadvocate.org
http://www.patientadvocate.org/

The Patient Advocate Foundation offers their services for free. Currently, they are a national non-profit organization that acts as a liaison for the patient. They help the patient resolve problems with their insurance company, employer and even their creditors. If you have a debilitating, or life threatening illness, this foundation can provide you with a case manager to help you with any difficulties that arise. As with most advocacy foundations, they also supply you with links to resources so you can help yourself, whether you are uninsured, underinsured or in need of financial assistance to pay everyday expenses related to your illness.

Along with the case management services I mentioned, they also provide educational materials and live chat services. I read one testimony that said the case manager set up a conference call with the doctor so they could ensure both the doctor and patient understood each other. I can think of many times that would have helped Donny and me.

They supply links to government pages so you can check on eligibility for disability benefits or if you are eligible for time off under the Family Leave Act. They also have a publication about appealing an insurance decision.

The foundation does not recommend doctors or give medical advice. One of the links they offer connects you with the American Medical Association website, at http://www.ama-assn.org. You can find a doctor according to specialty and geographic location but the AMA does not offer professional recommendations.

Although the foundation does not offer direct financial assistance, they do have a user friendly Resources tab on their website. Through this Resource tab you can get information on Healthcare Reform, along with directories for National Underinsured and Uninsured. They even have the National Financial Resource Directory which allows you to choose four areas in which you need financial assistance. If you are using the Resources tab, you can click on Medication Assistance and learn about the assistance programs offered by some of the pharmaceutical companies. They even have information on Employment discrimination, retention and other employment issues.

The foundation offers many free services in one convenient place. If you visit the foundation's frequently asked question area you will find **www.needymeds.com** mentioned as a resource for help with prescription costs. They offer a free discount prescription card with no hidden fees; they don't even require a registration process. As a matter of fact, you don't need to be a resident, you don't need to have insurance, and you don't need to fit into a certain income level. Any official prescription will be recognized, regardless of whether the medication is an over the counter drug or prescription only. You can share this card with friends, family and pets, yes, that's right. Even pet prescriptions are covered if written on a prescription blank.

AdvoConnection

PO Box 53
Baldwinsville, NY 13027
http://www.advoconnection.com/
If you have a question for an advocate, call the phone number listed for that Advocate

AdvoConnection supplies a directory for PRIVATE PAY advocates whose main focus and concern is your health. This is a new, unlicensed field where individuals get paid by you for their assistance during your medical need. Although they receive no reimbursement from the for-profit healthcare systems, like insurance companies, there may be some advocates who receive a commission for placing the patient in a certain nursing home or with some other service. This is one of the many reasons it is important to carefully interview prospective advocates. At www.advoconnection.com you will find a section with detailed suggestions on how to hire and interview an advocate.

In 2012, the Alliance of Professional Health Advocates developed a Code of Conduct and Professional Procedures based on the National Association of Health Advocacy

Consultants (NAHAC) original Code of Ethics written in 2010. Since this profession does not have national or international standards established, the Alliance recognized the importance of having a set of standardized procedures to help establish "integrity within this profession." You can view this Code of Conduct at their website. If you decide to hire an advocate, ask them if they follow this Code of Conduct and Professional Procedures.

These advocates can help in a variety of ways. If you don't see your specific need call and speak with an advocate listed in a close field to see if they can assist you. Here is a list of services listed on their website:

- Medical Assistance and Case Management
- Home Health and Eldercare Services
- End of Life Service
- Shared Decision Making
- Pain Management and Palliative Care*

    Palliative care focuses on the terminal patient's comfort.

- Mental Health/Substance Abuse Services
- Pregnancy, Birth and Pediatric Assistance
- Mediation Assistance for Family Health Matters
- Insurance/Payer Assistance
- Legal Assistance (Medical/Healthcare Related)
- Prevention Services

Each of these services has numerous subdivisions listed at www.advoconnection.com.

This site also suggests steps to take when considering hiring an advocate. They give you four steps to follow.

1. Decide on the services you need.
2. Search for an appropriate advocate.
3. Contact them.
4. Interview them.

They explain how to contact the individuals and explain that there is no limit to the number you may contact. Are you at a loss for what to ask during the interview? No problem. They offer a list of suggested questions. They even explain that the fees may vary between each advocate. They explain the different ways they may bill for their services: hourly, pay for a certain number of hours upfront, or by retainer are just a few ways they may handle their billing. They realize that if you are using their site your stress level may cause you to overlook details, so they even remind you to get everything in writing from the advocate you choose.

Several blogs, written by the Patient Advocates are also listed on this site.

These past two sites were general sites. Now I am going to get into some specific health issues and the support groups that are available to help you deal with them. I have put them in alphabetical order to make it easier to find the one you need.

ALZHEIMER'S DISEASE

Alzheimer's Association
National Office
225 N. Michigan Ave., Fl. 17
Chicago, IL 60601-7633
http://www.alz.org
Phone: 312-335-8700
PHONE: 1-800-272-3900--**24/7 Helpline** (information, referral or support)
TDD: 1-866-403-3073
EMAIL: info@alz.org

The Alzheimer's site offers many links including a link to a virtual library where you can search for and borrow available books and DVD's with pertinent information. They offer many other services, as well.

Services

- 24/7 Hotline services provided by professionals
    - "**Translation services available in 170 languages**"
- General information for patients, families, and caregivers
- Suggestions for handling financial and legal matters
- Information on Social Security Disability
- Information on insurance options

ALZHEIMER FOUNDATION OF AMERICA
322 Eight Avenue, 7th Floor
New York, NY 10001
Telephone: 1-866-232-8484--Toll-Free Hotline Hours: 9:00 a.m.-5:00 p.m. (ET)
                1-646-638-1542
Fax: 1-646-638-1546
Website: http://www.alzfdn.org

This is a national organization and their mission is to provide education and resources to help those in need. Their website, www.alzfdn.org, offers many user friendly links, including a link to find local resources. They provide educational resources to patients and medical personnel.

Services

- ➢ Toll Free Hotline-1-866-232-8484—available 9:00-5:00 (ET)
    - o Answered by trained Professionals
    - o Counseling by Licensed Social Workers
    - o Information and Nationwide Referrals to Community Resources

ARTHRITIS

Arthritis Foundation
National Office
1330 W. Peachtree Street
Suite 100
Atlanta, GA 30309
PHONE: 404-872-7100
WEBSITE: http://www.arthritis.org/
FACEBOOK: **Arthritis Foundation**
You Tube: **Arthritis Foundation**
FLICKR: **Arthritis-Foundation**

Visiting www.arthritis.org opens you eyes to the many different services offered by this foundation. They talk about the different types of arthritis, the political issues that may impact your life as a sufferer, and also have personal stories from arthritis sufferers.

Services

- Political Advocacy
- Research
- Patient Education

CANCER

American Cancer Society
National Home Office
250 Williams Street NW
Atlanta, GA 30303
Telephone: 800-227-2345 (24/7 for immediate answers)
TTY: 866-228-4327
Email: Through the website
Website: http://www.cancer.org

The American Cancer Society is probably the best known resource for information. They give you access to preventative steps, and information on finding cancer in its earliest stages. They work as legal advocates to get policies passed to make sure healthcare is available to everyone.

Donny had a great volunteer support person, who had survived pancreatic cancer, plus three bouts of lymphoma. This volunteer received training from the American Cancer Society. He helped Donny and I make informed medical decisions and helped Donny realize the possible harsh side effects of the treatments.

Services

- Toll-Free Hotline services
    - Trained Cancer Specialists
- Live Chat on Website
    - Monday-Friday 8:00 a.m. to 6:30 p.m. (CST)
- Political Advocacy
- Patient/Professional Education
- Patient Support
    - Rides to treatment
    - Online support communities

Association of Community Cancer Centers

11600 Nebel Street
Suite 201
Rockville, Maryland 20852-2557
PHONE: 301-984-9496
FAX: 301-770-1949
http://www.accc-cancer.org

Their website offers a membership directory featuring information on over 700 cancer programs located in many but not all states. The association focuses on education and research. Their long range goal is to "be recognized as the leading organization that advocates for quality comprehensive cancer care for all."

Services

- Directory of Cancer Programs for patients
- Topical Resource directory for providers

CancerConnect.com

WEBSITE: CancerConnect.com

This site is an award winning educational resource site for all types of cancer.

Services

- Health & Wellness Information

- Support for those newly diagnosed
- Resource listing by types of cancer
- Information on Cancer Treatment
- Tips for managing side effects
- Information on Cancer Screening
- Explanation of types of testing
- Clinical Trial information
- Dictionary listings for drugs and cancer
- Listing of support groups and other resources

Coalition of Cancer Cooperative Groups
Coalition to find Clinical Trials
Telephone: **1-877-227-8451** clinical trials matching service (a collaboration with the American Cancer Society)
Website: **http://www.cancertrialshelp.org**

This Coalition, a nonprofit organization, focuses on helping patients understand about cancer clinical trials. They strive to reach their goal of increasing patient awareness of, and participation in, cancer clinical trials. A variety of programs and information offered to medical personnel, patient advocates, and patients will help them to reach their goal.

I found the fact vs. myth section of their website very helpful. For instance, they cover the common myth that participants in cancer clinical trials are given sugar pills. They explain that contrary to this popular belief participants "are given the best cancer treatment options available or the chance to receive a new treatment being considered. Sugar pills (also called placebos) are rarely used in cancer clinical trials and are never used in place of treatment."

Services

- Links to find Clinical Trials near your home
- Cancer Clinical trial specialists available by phone
    - Monday-Friday 8:30 a.m. to 8:00 p.m. (EST)
    - Collaborative effort with the American Cancer Society
    - Glossary with Clinical Trial terminology
    - Patient Co-pay and Prescription assistance

National Comprehensive Cancer Network
275 Commerce Drive
Suite 300
Fort Washington, PA 19034
TELEPHONE: 215-690-0300

FAX: 215-690-0280
http://www.nccn.org

This alliance of leading cancer centers focuses on improving "the quality, effectiveness, and efficiency of cancer care so that patients can handle things themselves."

Services

- NCCN Guidelines for Patients is an easy to understand translation of the Physician guidelines.
- Dictionary of terms from those guidelines.
- Directory of Patient Advocacy and Support Organizations.
- Payment Assistance Information.
- Database of Actively Enrolling Clinical Trials.
- Video Library.

Pancreatic Cancer Support Group

The National Pancreas Foundation
3 Bethesda Metro Center, Suite 700
Bethesda, MD 20814
TELEPHONE: 301-961-1508
TOLL FREE: 866-726-2737
FAX: 301-657-9776
EMAIL: info@pancreasfoundation.org
WEBSITE: http://www.pancreasfoundation.org/

I found this support group on the general website of the National Pancreas Foundation. This website deals with numerous pancreatic illnesses. For the Pancreatic Cancer Support Group they teamed up with CancerConnect.com, a site which I noted earlier. If you go to www.CancerConnect.com and click on Types Of Cancer and then click on pancreatic you will find a lot of information.

But along with the Cancer Support Group the National Pancreas Foundation has information on numerous helpful resources including ones to help financially.

Services

- Listing of Financial Assistance Resources
- National Pancreas Clinical Trials Resource Center
- Link to be placed on Email Notification List for Clinical Trials
- Link for FDA drug approvals
- Directory of Research Centers
- Links to information on current research and clinical trial results
- Bookstore
- websites which offer information on diabetes

CARDIAC DISEASE

American Heart Association
7272 Greenville Avenue
Dallas, TX 75231
TELEPHONE: 800-242-8721
　　　　　　　888-474-8483 [Spanish]
WEBSITE: http://www.heart.org

This website offers information on stroke as well as heart disease. You will find nutrition tips, along with stress reduction advice and many other tips to keep you healthy. The site offers a section on the various types of cardiac disease and gives easy to understand descriptions of each. They also have a section for caregivers. Their resources are not limited to patients and caregivers; they also have a section for healthcare providers. Reminding us that a healthy heart starts early, they have a section geared toward educators.

Services

- ➢ Listing of Warning Signs
- ➢ Listing of award-winning, accredited and certified hospitals near you
- ➢ Listing of CPR Training centers
- ➢ Listing of locations to buy CPR and First Aid equipment

- On-line program, called "HEART360" to help you "understand and track the factors that affect your heart health.
- Political Advocacy

As you will see with the next program, men and women often present different symptoms when arriving at the emergency room for cardiac problems. You will notice the next group originated in 1999. This group helped to educate and make all of us aware of the unusual symptoms that a woman may experience.

Women Heart-The National Coalition for Women with Heart Disease

1100 17th Street, NW
Suite 500
Washington, DC 20036
TELEPHONE: 202-728-7199
SPANISH HOTLINE: 800-676-6002
FAX: 202-728-7238
EMAIL: mail@womenheart.org
WEBSITE: http://www.womenheart.org

This Coalition began in 1999 because of the lack of information available for women with heart disease. Unlike other organizations, "Women Heart" focuses solely on women's heart disease. This site offers educational and support services.

Services:

- Educational materials, including warning signs of heart attack
- Sister Match-A One on One support program that takes the time to match participants with compatible mentors. This program could be on-line, on the phone, in some cases even in person or a combination.

- List of Local Support Networks in 48 states
- Information on Co-pay prescription cards
- Information on Insurance
- Political Advocacy

American Stroke Association
7272 Greenville Avenue
Dallas, TX 75231
TELEPHONE: 800-242-8721
888-474-8483 [Spanish]
WEBSITE: http://www.strokeassociation.org

As you can see the most of the contact information is the same as for the American Heart Association, but they do have their own website. They focus on educational material and offer in-depth explanations of different types of strokes. The warning signs of a stroke are offered in several places, they even have a "Spot a Stroke" App for your cell phone. The best way to remember the warning signs is to think F.A.S.T. If you notice that one side of your face droops, or you notice arm weakness or numbness, or if you develop speaking difficulties, then it is time to call 911. You will also find a "Stroke Risk Quiz" on this website; this may give you a starting point to talk with your healthcare provider about how to reduce your risk factors. Similar to the American Heart Association site, http://www.heart.org, they offer a map where you can find recognized, accredited, and certified hospitals near you. They even have an explanatory list of the awards, accreditations and certifications, helping you once again to make an educated decision.

Services

- ➢ Support Group services list for patients and Caregivers
- ➢ Educational Material
- ➢ Political Advocacy
- ➢ Services offered in English, Spanish, Traditional Chinese, Simplified Chinese, Vietnamese

CELIAC DISEASE

CELIAC DISEASE FOUNDATION
National Office
Celiac Disease Foundation
20350 Ventura Boulevard
Suite 240
Woodland Hills, CA 91364
TELEPHONE: 818-716-1513 [9:30 a.m.-5:30 p.m. M-F Pacific Time]
INFORMATION REQUEST LINE: 818-716-1513 x105
WEBSITE: http://celiac.org/

Celiac Disease, an autoimmune disorder, which affects as many as 1 in 100 people worldwide. People with Celiac Disease cannot tolerate gluten, which can cause damage in the small intestine. This site, http://celiac.org, offers information on non-celiac gluten sensitivity as well as celiac disease. Their section on debunking the myths about celiac disease is enlightening. Did you know you could breathe in gluten? So even if you don't eat it, but you bake something non-gluten-free, it can affect you. Also, you should make sure your lip products are gluten-free because they are easily ingested.

Services

- List of Support Chapters by State
- Educational information
- List of gluten-free candy
- Link to find a health practitioner
- Link for Celiac Associations around the world
- Link for Celiac Policies around the world
- Explanation of Tax Deductions for the expense of buying gluten-free food
- Information on gluten-free diet

CROHN'S DISEASE

Crohn's & Colitis Foundation of America
733 Third Ave
Suite 510
New York, NY 10017
Telephone: 800-932-2423
EMAIL: info@ccfa.org
WEBSITE: http://www.ccfa.org/about/

The Crohn's and Colitis Foundation of America has an on-line support group as well as local support groups. They offer educational information on current research studies and how you can get involved, if you desire.

Services

- Fund research
- Offer patient webinars
- Offer links to find clinical studies
- Offer link to find local support groups
- Offer link to find health practitioner
- Political Advocacy opportunities

DIABETES

Diabetes Advocacy Alliance
WEBSITE: http://www.diabetesadvocacyalliance.org
Contact by email form on website

This alliance is a combination of non-profit agencies, health care providers and patients all working to improve the way diabetes is treated in the United States. Their focus lies in political advocacy.

Services

- Educational Webinars
- Links to members

PARKINSON'S DISEASE

American Parkinson's Disease Association
National Office [For Late In Life Onset]

135 Parkinson Avenue
Staten Island, NY 10305
TELEPHONE: 718-981-8001 [9:00 a.m. to 5:00 p. m. CST]
TOLL FREE: 800-223-2732
TOLL FREE HOTLINE: 800-457-6676

FAX: 718-981-4399
EMAIL: apda@apdaparkinson.org
WEBSITE: http://www.apdaparkinson.org/

This association focuses on patient services, research and education. They support a "national network of regional information and referral centers" as well as local support groups for patients, families and caregivers. This site, along with the website for the National Young Onset Center, is extremely user friendly and informative.

Services

- ➤ Toll Free Helpline covered by trained staff, Monday-Friday from 9 a.m.-5 p.m.
- ➤ Regional Information and Referral Centers-provide information on local services and educational material
- ➤ Support groups-nationwide network of local groups

- Chapters deal with fundraising but also coordinates services to support groups, offer educational seminars, recruit and support volunteers
- Political Advocacy

National Young Onset Center
25 N Winfield Road
Winfield, IL 60190
Phone: 877-223-3801
Fax: 630-933-4380
E-Mail: apda@youngparkinsons.org
Website: www.youngparkinsons.org

Although many of us may think of Parkinson's Disease as something that only hits older folks, at times it can hit younger adults. Young adults have different issues, and the American Parkinson's Disease Association has a special website to help them deal with these issues. One of the most helpful links on this website is the "Young Onset Resource Guide," an interactive resource offering sections on healthcare, physical and mental, insurance, employment and disability, financial, legal, and support services for the patient, the family and caregivers. They even have a special link for veterans.

Services

- ➢ Comprehensive guide to services available for younger patients and their families
- ➢ Extensive guide to veterans' services

- Information on symptoms, nutrition, treatments, and how to manage stress
- Newsletter
- Political Advocacy

CHAPTER 7-SUPPORT FOR CAREGIVERS

"…Living one day at a time;

Enjoying one moment at a time;

Accepting hardships as the pathway to peace…

That I may be reasonably happy in this life…"

-Excerpt from Serenity Prayer by Reinhold Niebuhr

A large part of Medical Advocacy is learning self-care. What happens when you are not the patient but the caregiver? As modern advancements in medicine increase our life expectancy, there are many people who are now "sandwiched" between caring for a chronically ill elderly family member and caring for their spouse and children. Where are the lines? When is it okay to say no? Many caregivers struggle with the question: who comes first the patient or the family? The caregivers rarely consider who is missing from that question: themselves. Now there is help for the helper. Agencies have formed that supply volunteers who can give caregivers a break. I will share information about a few national agencies in this chapter. The Medicare website, for one, has many links to help you find local assistance. Please don't hesitate to speak to your healthcare providers and local Senior Centers for suggestions.

WHAT DO I DO NOW THAT I'M A CAREGIVER

The AARP website contains a wealth of information. In their article entitled "8 Rules for New Caregivers," they give specific suggestions about how to make this difficult situation easier. Their suggestions include specific topics that should be discussed with the patient. Many times when dealing with seniors, talking about some of their wishes before the time of a medical emergency makes things run more smoothly. One of the frequently repeated rules, no matter what the source, deals with allowing the patient to make their own decisions for as long as possible. A nightmarish situation can evolve when a competent, elderly patient loses their voice in their own care.

From the beginning realistic limits should be in place on both sides. These limits help prevent misunderstandings and false expectations. As the caregiver you need to understand the delicate balance between assisting and hovering. The patient also needs to use fair judgment and not expect a 24 hour servant.

The necessity of organizational skills cannot be emphasized enough. Don't fret if the organization gene seems to have passed you by; now you can find help on the web, Check out www.lotsahelpinghands.com. They have easy to understand features that include calendars, places to keep vital information, message boards and a slew of other things to help you build your very own "helping community". So when you are setting your priorities, make sure to include Lotsa Helping Hands.

Never underestimate the power of personal contact when trying to set up a support network. At first you may think you need to do this by yourself, but most of us soon learn that being superwoman or superman only works in comic books. It may surprise you that people who haven't volunteered will eagerly assist you when you contact them personally. Think out of the box when looking for help; don't limit yourself to immediate family. Church members, neighbors, even workplace associates may step up when asked.

Are you one of those people who think delegation is an evil word? Does it conjure up visions of incomplete or imperfect assignments? Well, becoming a caregiver seems the perfect time to lose those old "tapes" running in your mind and move forward and see the bright light that can glow from delegation. According to http://www.thefreedictionary.com/, one definition of the word delegate means "to commit or entrust to another." Many people have a hard time delegating, some because they feel guilty for bothering others. When we look at this definition, it reminds us that delegating shows trust in the capabilities of others. Do you remember the feeling when someone trusted you enough to delegate something to you? Consider that the next time you say no to delegation.

Be creative and don't accept no from a family member without offering an alternative. When someone lives far away that does not preclude participation. We live in an age where banking and paying bills can all take place on-line. So be kind but firm in your request for assistance.

Long distances no longer preclude participation in regular family meetings either. You can use Skype or some other social networking source to have the family member present. If the technological age has done anything, it has made the world available at the touch of a keyboard. If your long distance family member does not have access to the web, use the telephone and have them participate that way.

Once everyone arrives be sure to have an agenda and some basic rules of order in place. Everyone reacts differently to change and having a loved one who requires care giving definitely fits into the change category. With the help of trained social workers family meetings can run smoothly and avoid much of the tension that arises during these times. Don't hesitate to look into this option as it may save the stability of the family.

There are some steps to take before you step into your role of caregiver. Talk to the person about housing options and preferences. Learn what social services and support organizations exist. Make sure you know the patient's medical history and document it. Know the contact information for the person's support network: church, friends, neighbors, pharmacist, anyone you can think of that may be able to assist you. Many people think you should not talk about finances; realize the need to break the silence and proceed with care. Medical and legal forms such as birth certificates, wills, advanced directives, insurance policies, and the deed to the home, just to name a few, should all be kept in a safe, accessible place and make sure all family members know where these important things are located.

HOW MEDICARE AND OTHERS CAN HELP CAREGIVERS

The Medicare website contains a wealth of information for patients and for caregivers. Go to http://www.medicare.gov/campaigns/caregiver/caregiver.html in order to begin your search of how to handle the healthcare maze without losing your sanity. This site covers questions about Medicare eligibility, how to handle expenses and even touches caregivers' self-care.

Let's start with caregivers support sites listed under www.eldercare.gov. This is sponsored by the U.S. Administration on Aging. This site allows you to find your specific needs easily. They have a locator based on zip code, city or topic. The topics include anything from Alzheimer's to Volunteerism, including a specific site for Caregivers. If you decide to choose topic first, the resulting site also has a locator option to find local resources in your area. You could also contact the U.S. Administration on Aging by phone at 1-800-677-1116.

Medicare.gov also offers suggestions on how to care for someone with a disability, chronic illness, or injury. Among other helpful suggestions they recommend you know your options. They explain that decisions should be left up to the patient whenever possible. If the patient has given you the right to make decisions for them, Medicare emphasizes the importance of asking questions about the possible outcomes and the various treatment options available, including home health care and how long will this care be necessary. Don't forget to investigate the cost of this care and how you will meet those costs. You will find a chapter on financial and budgeting help.

You can give the best care when you take care of yourself. The feelings of frustration and depression may sneak up on you. Don't be afraid to ask for help. That help may include one-on-one counseling for yourself or maybe a support group with others dealing with similar issues would give you the boost you need to keep going. Support Groups allow the members to share not only their difficulties but also their coping strategies. In this way the group may enlighten you even if you don't say a word. A caregiver educational workshop might fill your needs more than an ongoing support group. Often your local Agency on Aging or your local hospitals offers different programs with guest speakers dealing with specific topics of interest to caregivers. These groups generally allow for discussion after the presentation. Go to www.eldercare.gov to find local agencies and programs near you.

The National Caregivers Library, located at http://www.caregiverslibrary.org, seems particularly helpful. It offers numerous links dealing with housing, money and insurance, physical and emotional health, planning and assessment, along with record keeping and legal matters. They even deal with end of life issues. Unlike some other websites, this one also has contact information for those who don't want to deal with computers only. You can contact them by phone (804-327-1111), or by postal mail at 901 Moorefield Park Drive, Suite 100, Richmond, VA 23236.

In this technological age, support groups and educational groups also occur on-line. Check the website, http://www.caregiving.com/. The members of this site call themselves, "a community of family caregivers sharing stories, support and solutions about caring for a family member or friend." You can join this site for free. Podcasts, webinars, reading lists, a question and answer section, even an on-line store make up this website. They offer practical advice and provide a weekly "Care Plan" which includes reminders for self-care, along with caring for the other person. Apparently part of that self-care should include game time on the computer. Yes, they even offer some free games to help you unwind. The free "Virtual Caregiving Conference Webinar" has 2 versions, one for the family caregivers and one for the professionals working with family caregivers. Each current monthly webinar is free to everyone. Members also have free access to the archives; if not a member, you can purchase access to the archives for an annual fee of $9.95. They have a

Directory you can join so you can find others in your area. They also offer free eBooks on various subjects.

At some point in time you may ask, "Can I get paid for Caregiving?" Unfortunately a qualified maybe seems the only answer to that question. Many factors are taken into consideration and each state has different programs. If your patient is a senior citizen, the website www.payingforseniorcare.com/ offers invaluable information. What happens if your patient is younger? Go to http://www.patientadvocate.org/ for a treasure trove of information and hands on assistance. They offer arbitration, mediation and negotiation. They may even offer a 3 way phone call with providers to help you find the care your loved one needs.

The AARP website offers many different options for patients and caregivers. They reiterate the importance of self-care, providing the following 10 suggestions for stress busting:

1. "Put your physical needs first" remember to eat nutritious food, get sufficient sleep, look after your own physical and mental health
2. "Connect with friends" don't isolate yourself, schedule regular outings with positive friends and relatives
3. "Ask for help" make your To-Do list, then delegate. The secret of delegation involves the ability of the delegator not to micro-manage.
4. "Call on community resources" check the National Association of Professional Geriatric Care Managers** at http://www.caremanager.org/ to find a care manager near your loved one who could coordinate their care. These managers provide advocacy for all ages, not just senior citizens. You can also look into home health aides, house cleaning and home repair services. You do not have to do everything yourself.

5. "Take a break", you and your ailing loved one may benefit from a change. Check with friends or relatives to see if they can cover for you. If not them, check with home healthcare nurses, assisted living or nursing home facilities for short term care.
6. "Deal with your feelings" if you don't want to burden friends or family seek professional counseling or look for a support group, either on-line or in your community. Not dealing with your feelings will only cause you more problems.
7. "Find time to relax", do something you enjoy, such as, reading, walking, playing an instrument, whatever gives you some "down time". Remember the website http://www.caregiving.com/ even offers on-line games just to give you some break time.
8. "Get organized" prioritize your responsibilities; keep a calendar and your To-Do list handy.

Once again, http://www.caregiving.com/, can help with that by offering a weekly Care Plan.

9. "Just say no", most of us have to learn how to say no without feeling guilty. Know your limits and respect yourself enough to stay within those limits.

10. "Stay positive" and don't allow yourself to engage in any negative self-talk. Acknowledge all the positive things that you do. If your family has difficulties agreeing with care options there are elder care mediators* available in some locations. At www.eldercaremediators.com/ you will find a directory, along with information on how to select a mediator.

Elder mediation focuses on resolving conflicts related to aging that may block essential decisions.

CHAPTER 8-FINANCIAL ASSISTANCE

"Order: Let all your things have their places. Let each part of your business have its time."

Benjamin Franklin from *Poor Richard's Almanac*

When using the internet to find resources it is always important to know your source. If you Google "financial assistance for medical bills" you will get about 1,090,000 responses. The first source you want to look for is a government source. This may offer you resources you have already checked out, but it may also list others that are not as common. You also want to check the last date the site was updated.

As I did in Chapter 4, I will list any contact information available to make it as easy as possible for you to get the information and help you need.

The website http://answers.usa.gov is an official government web portal that covers many different areas of interest. In order to get information on financial assistance, click on FAQs on the top left corner of the screen. Enter "financial assistance for medical bills" in the search bar and then click on "Help with Medical Bills." This will bring up a page with eleven bulleted government resources plus additional information on Medicare/Medicaid assistance. The contact information for the Centers for Medicare and Medicaid Services follows:

Centers for Medicare & Medicaid Services
7500 Security Boulevard
Baltimore, MD 21244-1850
Telephone: 1-410-786-3000
Toll-Free: 1-877-267-2323
Website: http://www.medicare.gov

Another website you may find extremely helpful is the National Institute of Health. As a service of the National Library of Medicine, they have a website called Medline Plus. Medline Plus offers patients and their families reliable information about healthcare. For financial assistance information you would go to http://www.nlm.nih.gov/medlineplus. This is a user friendly site which gives you plenty of resources from which to choose. On their home page enter financial assistance in their search engine on the top right of the page. Many options will appear under financial assistance. Click on the first option labeled "Financial Assistance". This will bring you to their Financial

Assistance page and they have an option labeled "Start Here". Click on "Start Here" and it will take you to The National Genome Research Institute at http://www.genome.gov/11008842. This site breaks down the assistance into five specific categories. Some of the information is only links to other websites; I will only note the ones with direct contact information.

➢ Whenever you deal with the Internet please keep in mind, that sites frequently update their pages. When this happens you may view slightly different screens than I have listed. If you reach an updated site just use their search engines to look for your topic.

ASSISTANCE WITH PAYING FOR MEDICAL CARE AND PROCEDURES

The Department of Health and Human Services
200 Independence Avenue, S.W.
Washington, D.C. 20201
Telephone: 202-619-0257
Toll-free: 1-877-696-6775
Website: www.hhs.gov

Maternal and Child Health Bureau (MCHB)

Parklawn Building
Room 18-05
5600 Fishers Lane
Rockville, MD 20857
Phone: 301-443-2170
Fax: 301-443-1797
E-mail: ctibbs@hrsa.gov
Website: www.mchb.hrsa.gov

FINANCIAL AID FOR MEDICAL TREATMENT

Families USA
1201 New York Ave. NW
Suite 1100
Washington, DC 20005
Phone: 202-628-3030
Fax: 202-347-2417
E-mail: info@familiesusa.org
Website: www.familiesusa.org

National Patient Advocate Foundation
725 15th St. NW, Tenth Floor
Washington DC, 20005
Phone: 202-347-8009
Fax: 202-347-5579
E-mail: action@npaf.org
Website: www.npaf.org

Association of Maternal and Child Health Programs
230 M Street, NW
Suite 350
Washington, DC 20036
Phone: 202-775-0436
Fax: 202-775-0061
E-mail: info@amchp.org

Website: www.amchp.org

Patient Advocate Foundation
700 Thimble Shoals Boulevard
Suite 200
Newport News, VA 23606
Phone: 800-532-5274
Fax: 757-873-8999
E-mail: help@patientadvocate.org
Website: www.patientadvocate.org

ASSISTANCE WITH PAYING FOR MEDICATIONS

NORD's Medication Assistance Programs
National Organization for Rare Disorders
55 Kenosia Avenue
PO Box 1968
Danbury, CT 06813-1968
Toll-free: 800-999-6673 (voicemail only)
Phone: 203-744-0100
TDD: 203-797-9590
Fax: 203-798-2291
E-mail: orphan@rarediseases.org
Website: www.rarediseases.org

ASSISTANCE WITH INSURANCE ISSUES

Health Care Choices
P.O. Box 21039
Columbus Circle Station
New York, NY 10023
Toll-free: 800-368-5779

PARTICIPATION IN CLINICAL TRIALS

Patient Recruitment and Public Liaison Office
NIH Clinical Center

Bethesda, MD 20892-2655
Toll-free: 800-411-1222
Fax: 301-480-9793
E-mail: prpl@mail.cc.nih.gov
Website: www.cc.nih.gov

GLOSSARY

- **Ayurvedic**-the conventional Hindu system of medicine, founded chiefly on naturopathy and homeopathy. http://medical-dictionary.thefreedictionary.com

- **Care Manager Services**-Work with all ages to provide comprehensive assessments and help the families plan for current and future needs of loved ones. http://www.caremanager.org/why-care-management/what-you-should-know/advocacy-for-all-ages-care-management-is-not-just-for-seniors/

- **Chemotherapy**-Chemotherapy is treatment of cancer with anticancer drugs. http://medical-dictionary.thefreedictionary.com

- **Chinese medicine**-*n* 1. (Medicine) a traditional system of medical treatment based on the principles of Yin and

Yang, involving such treatments as acupuncture and the use of a range of drugs derived from animal and vegetable sources. http://medical-dictionary.thefreedictionary.com

- **CT SCAN-**The abbreviated term for computed or computerized axial tomography. The test may involve injecting a radioactive contrast into the body. Computers are used to scan for radiation and create cross-sectional images of internal organs. http://medical-dictionary.thefreedictionary.com

- **Elder Care Mediator-**Elder mediation focuses on resolving conflicts related to aging that may block essential decisions. These disputes may involve squabbling adult siblings or other family members. Or arguments may occur with a private caregiver or between residents in a retirement community. http://www.eldercaremediators.com/

- **Medical Journal-**A personal record (*focusing on medical issues*) of occurrences, experiences, and reflections kept on a regular basis. (*Emphasis added*) http://www.thefreedictionary.com/

- **Palliative Care-**Non-curative comfort care provided to the dying or to people terminally ill with an incurable disease. It focuses on relieving pain and distressing symptoms and addresses physical, emotional, social and spiritual needs. http://medical-dictionary.thefreedictionary.com/

- **Pancreaticoduodenectomy-**Removal of all or part of the pancreas along with the duodenum. Also known as "**Whipple's procedure**" or "Whipple's operation." http://medical-dictionary.thefreedictionary.com

- **PT Scan-**A positron emission tomography (PET) scan is an imaging test that uses a radioactive substance called a tracer to look for disease in the body. A PET scan shows *how organs and tissues are working.* This is different than magnetic resonance imaging (MRI) and computed tomography (CT), which show the structure of and blood flow to and from organs. http://www.nlm.nih.gov/medlineplus/ency/article/003827.htm

- **Radiation Therapy-** sometimes called radiotherapy, x-ray therapy radiation treatment, cobalt therapy, electron beam therapy, or irradiation uses high energy, penetrating waves or particles such as x rays, gamma rays, proton rays, or neutron rays to destroy cancer cells or keep them from reproducing.
    http://medical-dictionary.thefreedictionary.com

- **Whipple Procedure**-a radical pancreatoduodenectomy with removal of the distal third of the stomach, the entire duodenum, and the head of the pancreas, with gastrojejunostomy, choledochojejunostomy, and pancreatic jejunostomy. This procedure is used for pancreatic carcinoma. http://medical-dictionary.thefreedictionary.com

- **Wound Vac Therapy--Vacuum Assisted Closure (VAC)**-trademark for a system that uses the controlled negative pressure of a vacuum to promote healing of certain types of wounds. The edges of the wound are made airtight with foam and a dressing, and a tube is placed in the wound, connecting to a canister that creates a vacuum. Infectious materials and other fluids are then sucked out of the wound. http://medical-dictionary.thefreedictionary.com